AI Starter Guide

Understanding Artificial Intelligence for Young Learners

Amaara Verma & Abeer Verma

Fusion Books

Publisher	:	**Fusion Books** X-30, Okhla Industrial Area, Phase-II New Delhi-110020
Phone	:	011- 40712200
E-mail	:	wecare@diamondbooks.in
Website	:	www.diamondbooks.in
Edition	:	2026

Author's Note

Artificial Intelligence may sound like a complicated idea — something meant only for scientists, engineers, or grown-ups working in big companies.

But the truth is simple:

AI is already part of your world.

When you unlock your phone with your face, when YouTube recommends a video you like, or when a learning app adjusts questions to your level — you are interacting with AI.

As students growing up in a digital age, we began asking an important question:

If children are already using AI every day, shouldn't they understand it too?

This book was created as a starter guide — a first step into understanding how machines learn, how data works, and how AI quietly shapes our lives.

Abeer enjoys breaking things down into simple steps — explaining how AI works and how machines learn from patterns.

Amaara likes asking deeper questions — why AI matters, how it should be used responsibly, and how it will affect our future.

Together, we believe that learning about AI should begin early — in a way that is simple, safe, and inspiring.

This book is not about making you an expert overnight.

It is about helping you ask better questions.

Because every big innovation begins with curiosity.

Let your AI journey begin.

— Abeer & Amaara Verma

Preface

Why Young Learners Should Understand AI
Artificial Intelligence is no longer a futuristic idea. It is part of everyday life.
From smart assistants and recommendation apps to online learning tools and games, AI is shaping how children learn, play, and explore the world.

Yet many students are taught how to use devices — but not how those devices think.
AI Starter Guide is written especially for young learners who are curious about technology and want to understand it in simple language.

Inside this book, you will discover:
- What Artificial Intelligence really means
- How AI learns from data
- Where AI is used in daily life
- How AI is helping India grow
- What jobs AI may create in the future
- Why fairness, safety, and ethics matter

Aligned with the spirit of NEP 2020 and future-ready education, this guide encourages students to think critically, explore responsibly, and imagine creatively.

AI is not something to fear.
It is something to understand.
And understanding begins with simple questions.

Foreword

We are living in a time when technology evolves faster than ever before.
Artificial Intelligence has moved from research laboratories into homes, classrooms, hospitals, farms, and smartphones. It influences how we communicate, learn, travel, and solve problems.

For young learners growing up in this environment, understanding AI is becoming as important as learning mathematics or science.
AI Starter Guide offers a thoughtful and age-appropriate introduction to this powerful technology. It explains complex ideas in simple language, encourages curiosity, and highlights the importance of ethical responsibility.

Most importantly, it reminds us that technology must always serve humanity — not replace it.
By combining clarity, imagination, and responsibility, this book empowers children to become informed digital citizens and future innovators.

Artificial Intelligence may shape the future —
but young minds will shape how it is used.

Let this be the beginning of many thoughtful conversations about AI in homes and classrooms across the country.

Table of Contents

Chapter 1

What is Artificial Intelligence?

Have you ever asked your phone to play your favorite song? Or seen YouTube recommend videos you love to watch? Maybe you've used Google Maps to find the fastest way to school? If yes, then you've already met Artificial Intelligence, or as we call it, AI!

But what is this "AI"? Is it a robot? Is it magic? Or is it something else?

Let's explore this new friend together.

What Does "Artificial Intelligence" Mean?

To understand Artificial Intelligence, let's break the term into two parts:

- Artificial means something made by humans, not natural.
- Intelligence means the ability to think, learn, and make decisions.

So, Artificial Intelligence is when machines (like computers, robots, or apps) are made to think and learn like humans.

It's like giving a brain to a computer!

Can Machines Really Think?

Let's play a small game.
Imagine you have a robot named Buddy. If you ask Buddy, "What's 9 times 6?", and it says "54" instantly, is that thinking?
Well, Buddy didn't guess. It learned from many examples before.
It remembered the answer, just like you did in school. That's how AI works — it learns from data (lots of information), practices with examples, and gets better.
Machines don't have feelings, but they can be trained to recognize patterns and respond smartly.

AI vs. Human Brain

Here's a fun comparison:

Activity	Human Brain	AI/Computer Brain
Learning a language	By listening and speaking	By reading tons of texts
Playing chess	By thinking ahead	By calculating all possibilities
Recognizing faces	By memory and emotion	By scanning facial features

Your brain is creative and emotional. AI is fast and logical — but it doesn't dream or feel.

What Can AI Do?

Today, AI can do many things such as:
- Answering questions (like ChatGPT or Alexa)
- Recognizing photos (tagging faces in pictures)
- Helping doctors (reading X-rays to find illness)

- Teaching students (custom learning apps)
- Driving cars (self-driving technology!)

Imagine if you had a personal assistant that never sleeps — that's how powerful AI can be.

Is AI New or Old?

You may think AI is a recent idea, but people started dreaming about smart machines more than 70 years ago! A man named Alan Turing in the 1950s asked, "Can machines think?" That's when the journey began. But it's only in the last 10–15 years that AI has become a part of our everyday lives — thanks to smartphones, the internet, and fast computers.

Where Do We Use AI Every Day?

You might not even notice, but AI is all around you:

- When your phone suggests emojis or autocorrects a word
- When YouTube recommends videos you like
- When food delivery apps guess your order
- When Google Maps tells you the fastest way
- Even when your photos get automatically grouped by face or place!

Why Should You Learn About AI?

You are growing up in a world where AI will shape your future. Tomorrow's teachers, farmers, doctors, artists — all will use AI in some way.

Understanding how AI works will help you:

- Be a smart user of technology
- Stay safe online
- Solve real-life problems
- Become a creator, not just a consumer of tech

It's not just for engineers — AI is for everyone!

Quick Recap

Let's remember what we learned:

Concept	Meaning
Artificial	Made by humans
Intelligence	The ability to think and solve problems
AI =	Machines that learn and make smart decisions
Uses of AI	Phones, games, hospitals, schools, maps
Future with AI	Jobs, safety, learning, solving big problems

Try It Yourself!

1. **Look around your house** – Can you spot 3 things that may be using AI? (Hint: Think phones, TVs, apps!)
2. **Talk to your parents** – Ask them if they've used AI without knowing it.
3. **Imagine** – If you had an AI robot, what job would you give it?

Thought of the Day:

"AI is not just science fiction anymore. It's science fact – and it's part of your world!"

Starter Insight

Abeer Explains:
AI is not magic. It works using patterns and data — just like learning from examples.
Amaara Asks:
If AI learns from us, what kind of examples should we give it?

Chapter 2

The 5Ws of Artificial Intelligence

Have you ever been curious and asked questions like:

- What is this?
- Why does it work this way?
- When did it start?
- Where do I see it?
- Who made it?

These five powerful questions are called the 5Ws, and they help us understand any new topic — even something as big and exciting as Artificial Intelligence (AI)!

Let's break it down:

1. What is AI?

We learned in Chapter 1 that Artificial Intelligence means machines that can think, learn, and make smart decisions, just like humans — but without feelings.

But there's more:

AI can be found in software (like Google Search), in apps (like Duolingo or Spotify), or in machines (like smart speakers or cleaning robots).
Think of AI as your helpful digital assistant — it listens, learns, and acts!

Quick Example:
When you search "best birthday cake designs" online, AI helps sort millions of results to show the ones you'll probably like the most.

2. Why Was AI Created?

Great question!
AI was created to help humans do things faster, better, and smarter. Sometimes, tasks are too difficult, boring, or time-consuming for people to do alone.

Here are a few reasons why AI is useful:

- To solve big problems (like climate change, traffic jams, or medical diagnosis)
- To save time (like online shopping or translating languages)
- To make life easier (like reminders, maps, and voice search)

Think about this: Would you want a robot to help with your homework? Or remind you to drink water? That's why we need AI — it's like having an extra brain that never gets tired!

3. When Did AI Begin?

AI might feel new, but the idea has been around for a long time.

Here's a short timeline:

Year	What Happened?
1950s	Alan Turing asked: "Can machines think?"
1960s–80s	Early computers learned to play games and solve puzzles
1997	A computer (Deep Blue) beat a chess champion!
2010s	AI entered our phones, homes, schools
2020s	AI became part of daily life in India and beyond

So, AI has been growing slowly — but today, it's everywhere!

4. Where Is AI Used?

Let's explore some real places where AI is working today:

At Home:
- Smart TVs suggest shows
- Voice assistants set alarms
- Security cameras detect motion

At School:
- Learning apps adjust to your speed
- Language tools help with grammar
- Educational robots assist in science labs

In Hospitals:
- AI helps doctors read X-rays
- Tracks health through wearables
- Chatbots answer patient questions

In Farms:
- AI predicts weather
- Checks soil quality
- Suggests the right time to water crops

On Roads:

- Google Maps guides traffic
- Self-driving cars (still being tested)
- Sensors in smart traffic lights

India is using AI in areas like railways, weather prediction, banking, and farming. So AI is not just in big cities — it's helping villages and towns too!

5. Who Makes AI?

AI doesn't appear like magic. It's built by people just like you — students, teachers, scientists, and engineers.

Some important roles:

- Data scientists feed examples to machines
- AI engineers write codes and build models
- Designers make sure AI is helpful and fair
- Ethics experts check if AI is safe to use

Fun Fact: Some school students in India have even built their own AI apps using simple tools like Scratch and Teachable Machine!

The Future Needs YOU!

AI is changing how we live, learn, and work. And tomorrow, you could be the one designing new kinds of AI:

- A robot that teaches yoga?
- An app that helps farmers detect crop disease?
- A smart chair that reminds grandparents to stretch?

It all begins with asking questions — just like the 5Ws!

Quick Recap

W	Meaning
What	AI is machines that learn and make decisions
Why	To help humans solve problems faster and smarter
When	Started in 1950s, growing faster in 2020s
Where	Homes, schools, farms, hospitals, everywhere!
Who	Created by engineers, scientists — and YOU!

Try It Yourself!

- Write down the 5Ws of something you love (like football, painting, or cartoons).
- Then write the 5Ws of AI in your own words — show your teacher or parents!

Thought of the Day:

"Great learners ask great questions. And AI begins with five simple ones — What, Why, When, Where, and Who!"

Chapter 3

How Does AI Work?

Now that you know what Artificial Intelligence is and why it matters, you might be wondering:

"How does AI actually work?"
"Can machines really learn?"
"How does a computer know what I want?"

Let's break it down, step by step — like peeling an orange!

Step 1: AI Learns from Data

Imagine your friend has never seen a mango before. But if you show them 100 pictures of mangoes and say "These are mangoes," guess what? Your friend will begin to recognize them in real life!

That's what AI does too.
AI needs data to learn. Data is just a fancy word for information.

For example:

- A music app needs data on which songs you like
- A chatbot learns from thousands of questions and answers
- A robot vacuum collects data on your room's layout

Fun Analogy:
AI is like a sponge — it soaks up data and learns patterns.

Step 2: AI Looks for Patterns

After gathering data, AI tries to find patterns.
Let's say you eat chocolate every Sunday. If an AI looks at your weekly snack log

It might learn:
"Aha! This person eats chocolate every Sunday. Let me remind them next time."
Pattern = habit = prediction!

Another example: When you type "Good m…" in a text, your phone suggests "Good morning!" That's AI noticing patterns in how people talk.

Step 3: AI Practices and Learns

Just like you need practice to get better at math or drawing, AI also trains.

This process is called machine learning — teaching machines to learn from examples.

Types of learning:

1. **Supervised Learning:** Like a teacher helping a student. The AI is shown the question and the right answer.
   - o E.g., "This is a cat. That's a dog."

2. Unsupervised Learning: The AI explores on its own and tries to group things.

- o E.g., It notices pictures with wheels go together (vehicles).

3. Reinforcement Learning: The AI learns from trying — and failing!

- o Like a game where it earns points for doing the right thing.

Example: AI learning to play a video game gets better with every try — just like you do.

Step 4: AI Makes Smart Decisions

Once trained, AI begins to make decisions. Not magical guesses — but based on what it has seen and learned.

- A shopping app shows you a red shirt because you looked at red shoes earlier.
- A spell checker corrects "recieve" to "receive" because it knows the right spelling.
- A smart fridge suggests recipes based on the food inside!

AI doesn't "think" like you. It uses logic and rules to choose the best option from what it knows.

Let's Build a Simple AI Example:

Let's imagine you want to create a "SnackBot" — an AI robot that gives you snack suggestions.

Here's how it would work:

Step	What Happens
1	SnackBot gathers data: What snacks you eat, when
2	It finds patterns: You love fruit on weekdays

3	It learns: Monday = apple, Friday = chips
4	**It decides:** Suggests banana on Monday afternoon

Your robot is now smart because you trained it!

But AI Isn't Perfect...

Sometimes, AI can make mistakes, especially if:

- It didn't learn from enough examples
- The data it learned from was wrong or confusing
- The situation is completely new

That's why AI is not a replacement for humans. It's a tool to help us — not to think for us.

Real-Life Tools That Use This Learning Process:

Tool or App	What It Learns From
YouTube	Videos you watch
Google Maps	Traffic data from thousands of drivers
Face ID	Pictures of your face
Language Apps	Words you use often
Shopping Apps	What you browse and buy

Quick Recap

Concept	What It Means
Data	Information AI learns from
Pattern	Repeated behavior AI notices
Machine Learning	AI improving by practicing
Decision Making	AI choosing the best answer from patterns

Try It Yourself!

1. Keep a snack journal for 7 days.
What do you eat each day? Try to find your own pattern!

2. Think like an AI:
If your friend eats bananas on Monday and popcorn on Friday, what would you suggest on Wednesday?

3. AI Game:
Create "If-then" rules for yourself.

- o If it's sunny, wear sunglasses.
- o If I'm sleepy, play music.

That's how AI makes rules too!

Thought of the Day:

"AI learns just like we do — through examples, practice, and a little bit of curiosity!"

Starter Insight

Abeer Explains:
Machine learning means improving through practice — not through emotions.
Amaara Asks:
If AI keeps improving, how do we make sure it improves in the right direction?

Chapter 4

AI in Our Daily Life

You've learned what AI is and how it works. Now it's time to look around you — because Artificial Intelligence is everywhere!
It's not just in robots or high-tech labs. AI is in your home, your phone, your classroom — even in your favorite apps.
Let's explore where AI lives in your everyday world.

AI at Home

You don't have to go far to find AI. Just pick up your phone or talk to your smart speaker!

Here are some ways AI helps you at home:

- **Voice Assistants like Alexa, Siri, and Google Assistant can:**
  - Answer questions like "What's the capital of France?"
  - Set alarms, reminders, and timers
  - Tell jokes or play your favorite song

- **Smart TVs use AI to:**
  - o Recommend shows you might enjoy
  - o Automatically adjust brightness and volume
  - o Understand your voice when you say "Play cartoons"

- **Home Security systems use AI to:**
  - o Recognize faces at the door
  - o Detect unusual movement
  - o Send alerts to your family's phone

Fun Fact: If your refrigerator reminds you to buy milk, it's using AI!

AI at School

Yes, AI is even helping you learn better — sometimes quietly in the background!

- **Learning Apps like BYJU'S, Khan Academy, or Duolingo:**

o Adjust lessons to match your speed
o Repeat difficult topics until you master them
o Use AI to track your strengths and weaknesses

- **Smart Classrooms:**

o Projectors that respond to voice
o Attendance using facial recognition
o AI tutors that explain tough problems step-by-step

- **Spelling and Grammar Tools:**

o Suggest corrections when you write emails or essays
o Help you write better sentences

Think about this: Has your app ever said "Well done!" when you got a question right? That's AI cheering for you!

AI in Your Phone

Your smartphone is like a mini-AI lab in your pocket.

Here's what it can do:

- **Predict Text:** Finishes your sentence as you type
- **Face Unlock:** Uses AI to recognize your face
- **Camera Filters:** Detect your face and apply cute ears or hats!
- **Maps & Navigation:** Suggests the fastest route using traffic data
- **Photo Albums:** Groups photos by person or place using face detection

AI is helping your phone understand you better — your voice, habits, likes, and needs.

AI in Shopping and Food

Do you like ordering food online or shopping for cool gadgets?

AI plays a role here too:

- **Food apps** (like Swiggy or Zomato) learn your favorite dishes and suggest what you might want next.
- **Shopping sites** (like Amazon or Flipkart) recommend products based on what you've browsed or bought before.
- **AI chatbots** on websites answer your questions instantly, even at midnight!

Example: If you love mango ice cream and search for it once, next time the app may suggest mango shake too!

AI in Games and Entertainment

Ever played a video game where the enemies get smarter every level? That's AI at work!

- **Video Games:**

o Enemies learn your tricks and get harder to beat
o AI controls characters you don't play

- **Music Apps:**

o Spotify or YouTube Music suggest songs based on your mood or time of day

- **Streaming Services:**

o Netflix or Disney+ show movie suggestions using your viewing history

Challenge: Try noticing when a game character changes its behavior — it may be learning from you.

AI in Health and Safety

AI also helps us stay safe and healthy, even if we don't notice it.

- Smartwatches track your heart rate, steps, and sleep
- AI in hospitals helps doctors read scans and test results
- Emergency apps use AI to detect car accidents or sudden falls

AI can help save lives — especially when used with care and responsibility.

AI in the World Around You

AI doesn't just live in gadgets — it helps make the world better too:

- **Farming:**

o AI sensors check soil health
o Predict rainfall or pests

- **Transport:**

o Self-driving cars (still being tested)
o Smart traffic lights reduce jams

- **Environment:**
    - o AI monitors pollution levels
    - o Helps scientists track endangered animals

So, whether it's a big city or a small village — AI is quietly helping humans do more, faster, and smarter.

Quick Recap

Where You See AI	What It Does
Home	Listens to commands, adjusts smart devices
School	Personalizes learning, automates attendance
Phone	Suggests words, unlocks, organizes photos
Shopping	Recommends products, chats with customers
Games & Apps	Makes gameplay smarter, recommends media
Healthcare	Tracks health, helps doctors read data
Farming/Traffic	Makes agriculture and roads more efficient

Try It Yourself!

1. **Make a list:** Can you find 5 things you did today that used AI? (Hint: Phone, food, class, game…)

2. **Ask someone at home:** "How do you think AI helps you?" Share their answer in class!

3. **Start a "Spot the AI" notebook:** Write one new AI example every day for a week.

Thought of the Day:

"AI is not just in robots. It's in your pocket, your classroom, your games — and your future."

Starter Insight

Abeer Explains:
Your phone becomes smarter the more you use it.
Amaara Asks:
Is your phone learning from you — or are you adapting to it?

Chapter 5

AI for India's Progress

India is a land of farmers, teachers, scientists, doctors, shopkeepers, and students like you. From the smallest village to the biggest city, people are working hard to build a better tomorrow.

But did you know that Artificial Intelligence (AI) is now helping them? Yes! AI is becoming one of India's most powerful tools for growth and progress.
Let's explore how AI is being used across different areas in India to solve real problems and create exciting new opportunities.

AI in Agriculture: Helping Our Farmers

More than half of India's people depend on farming. But farmers face challenges like unpredictable weather, pests, poor soil, and low prices.

That's where AI steps in:
- **Weather prediction:** AI uses satellite data to tell when it will rain, helping farmers decide the right time to sow or harvest.

- **Soil health:** AI tools test soil and tell farmers which crops will grow best.
- **Pest control:** AI can spot crop diseases using pictures from phones or drones, and suggest natural treatments.
- **Market prices:** AI apps help farmers know where they can sell their produce at the best rate.

Real Story: A mobile app called Kisan AI is being used in parts of India to help farmers get real-time advice in their own language!

AI in Education: Smarter Learning for All

India has millions of children in schools — in cities, towns, and remote villages. AI is helping bring quality education to everyone, everywhere.

Here's how:

- **Personalized learning:** AI-powered apps adjust the speed of learning to match each child's level.
- **Local languages:** AI helps translate lessons so students can learn in their mother tongue.
- **Teacher support:** AI tools help teachers track student progress and give extra help where needed.
- **Remote learning:** In places where there are no teachers, AI tutors can explain subjects clearly through videos and quizzes.

Real Story: In Andhra Pradesh, AI is being used to predict which students might drop out of school — so that teachers can support them early and help them stay in school.

AI in Healthcare: Saving Lives with Smart Tools

India is a large country, and not every place has easy access to doctors. AI is now helping people stay healthier by reaching even the most remote areas.

Here's how AI is helping in health:
• **Disease detection:** AI reads medical scans (like X-rays and MRIs) and can spot problems early.
• **Online check-ups:** Chatbots and apps ask questions and guide patients about next steps.
• **Medicine discovery:** AI helps scientists create new medicines faster.
• **Wearables:** Devices like smartwatches track heart rate, steps, and sleep, and warn users of any unusual changes.

Real Story: In Bengaluru, an AI system helped detect breast cancer in patients much earlier than traditional tests. That means better chances of recovery.

AI in Transport and Safety: Smarter Cities

India's roads, traffic, and transport systems are getting busier every year. AI is making them safer and more efficient.

Some ways AI is helping:
• **Smart traffic lights:** AI adjusts signal timings based on how crowded a road is.
• **Accident alerts:** Cameras and sensors alert police about accidents quickly.
• **Public transport:** AI tracks buses and trains to avoid delays and crowding.
• **Facial recognition:** Used in airports and railway stations for faster check-ins and security.

Real Story: In Delhi, AI is used to manage traffic signals, which has helped reduce waiting times and pollution at busy junctions.

AI in Business: Helping Shops and Startups

From big online stores to tiny local businesses, AI is helping people grow their work:

• **Customer support:** Chatbots answer questions and take orders anytime.
• **Product suggestions:** AI shows customers what they're most likely to buy.
• **Inventory tracking:** AI helps shopkeepers manage stock and avoid losses.
• **Loan approvals:** Banks use AI to decide quickly if someone can get a loan.

Real Story: Small shopkeepers using JioMart get AI support to understand what's selling best in their area — and what they should stock up on.

AI in Space and Science: Exploring the Universe

India is also using AI for big dreams — like going to space!
• ISRO, India's space agency, is using AI to plan satellite launches and analyze space data.
• Robots are being trained to assist astronauts and perform tasks in space.
• AI is helping scientists understand climate change, earthquakes, and even wildlife patterns.

Real Story: India's Chandrayaan-3 moon mission used AI to process surface data and guide its lunar lander safely — making India the first country to land on the moon's south pole!

India's National AI Mission

The Indian government has launched the "National AI for All" strategy. Its goals are:
• To make AI accessible in every Indian language
• To use AI in health, education, farming, and justice
• To create jobs in AI-based careers
• To teach AI from school level (just like this book!)

India's vision is not just to use AI — but to lead the world in using AI for good.

Quick Recap

Sector	How AI Helps India
Agriculture	Predicts weather, checks soil, detects pests
Education	Personalizes learning, supports teachers
Healthcare	Diagnoses diseases, supports remote care
Transport	Manages traffic, improves safety
Business	Helps small shops and big companies grow
Space & Science	Assists in missions and research

Try It Yourself!

1. **Pick one area** (like farming, school, or shopping) and write 3 ways AI can help improve it.
2. **Interview a grown-up:** Ask them how they think AI is changing India.
3. **Imagine:** If you had to create one AI tool to help your village, town, or school — what would it do?

Thought of the Day:

"AI is not just changing the world — it's changing your world, right here in India."

Chapter 6

AI and the Jobs of Tomorrow

Close your eyes for a moment and imagine this:
You wake up one morning in the year 2040. Your room lights up automatically. A friendly AI assistant reads your homework notes aloud while your clothes are ironed by a robot. At school, your lessons are customized just for you. After class, you work on a science project — designing an AI to clean up rivers!

Sounds exciting?
This isn't science fiction. This is a glimpse of your future, and Artificial Intelligence (AI) will be a big part of it.

AI is Changing Jobs — Not Replacing Everyone

Many people worry: "Will AI take away jobs?"
Here's the truth: AI will change jobs, not take them all away.

- Some jobs will disappear (like humans doing routine data entry).
- Some jobs will change (like farmers using AI to check crops).
- And many new jobs will be born — jobs that didn't exist before!

Just like we once shifted from riding bullock carts to flying planes, our work is evolving too — and AI is a new tool, not a threat.

Jobs That Use AI Today

Let's look at how different fields are using AI already:

Field	AI Helps With...
Medicine	Diagnosing diseases, creating new medicines
Education	Personalized learning, virtual tutors
Agriculture	Monitoring crops, predicting weather
Transport	Self-driving vehicles, traffic control
Media	Writing news summaries, editing videos
Sports	Analyzing performance, predicting injuries
Banking	Detecting fraud, managing savings
Space	Robot navigation, space missions

In all of these, humans and AI work together to get better results.

Careers of the Future: AI + You!

Here are some amazing jobs that may interest you — and they all involve AI:

1. AI Engineer
Designs and builds intelligent systems that solve problems.

2. Data Scientist
Finds patterns in data and helps businesses make smart decisions.

3. Robot Designer
Creates robots that walk, talk, clean, or even explore space!

4. AI Doctor Assistant
Helps doctors by analyzing test results quickly and accurately.

5. Smart City Planner
Uses AI to make cities cleaner, safer, and better for people.

6. AI Artist or Musician
Creates songs, paintings, or animations using AI tools.

7. AI Teacher or Curriculum Designer
Builds learning tools that adapt to each student's style and speed.

Note: These careers combine creativity, logic, and curiosity — not just coding.

AI Needs Everyone — Including You!

AI is not just for boys or computer nerds. It's for:

- Girls and boys
- Students from big cities or small villages
- People who love science OR art
- Everyone who asks "what if?" and "how?"

India's future in AI needs children who:

- Understand their local problems
- Think creatively
- Use technology with kindness and care

Skills to Start Learning Now

You don't have to wait till college. Start small — start today!

Logical Thinking

- Play puzzle games and brain teasers
- Break big problems into small steps

Creativity

- Draw, design, or invent your own robot ideas
- Write stories or comics about the future

Communication

- Practice explaining big ideas in simple words
- AI jobs need teamwork and clear thinking!

Basic Coding

- **Try kid-friendly tools like:**
  - o Scratch
  - o Code.org
  - o Google Teachable Machine

Even if you don't want to be an engineer, these skills help in almost every job today.

Real Kids Doing Real AI!

• Tanmay Bakshi, from Canada (with Indian roots), started coding at age 5. He now helps companies build AI systems!

• Girls Who Code is a global group teaching young girls to build apps and robots — and change the world.

If they can do it, so can you.

Quick Recap

Question	**Answer**
Will AI take away jobs?	No - it will change them and create new ones
What kind of jobs?	In health, farming, education, art, and more
Who can work with AI?	Everyone — boys, girls, artists, dreamers!

How to start?	Learn thinking, creating, coding, and teamwork

Try It Yourself!

1. **Draw a job of the future.** Will you be a robot teacher, a farm drone pilot, or a space scientist?
2. **Interview a grown-up** about how their job has changed with technology.
3. **Start a career journal:** Every time you hear of a cool AI-related job, write it down!

Thought of the Day:

"AI is not taking over the world — it's inviting you to help build it."

Starter Insight

Abeer Explains:
AI changes how we work — it doesn't replace human creativity.
Amaara Asks:
What human skill will always remain important, no matter how smart AI becomes?

Chapter 7

The Good and Bad of AI (Ethics & Safety)

Imagine you have a superpower: you can listen to every conversation in the world and suggest what people should say next. That's a little like what AI can do.
But should you use that superpower all the time? Should you listen in without permission? Should you treat everyone the same, no matter their name or language?
These are big questions, and in this chapter, we'll explore something called AI ethics — the study of what is right and wrong when we use Artificial Intelligence.

Because just like superheroes, AI needs rules.

What Is Ethics?

Ethics means doing what is right, fair, and good — even when no one is watching.

When we use AI, we have to think about:

- Is it being fair to everyone?
- Is it protecting people's privacy?
- Is it used for helping, not hurting?
- Does it give humans the final say?

These are not just adult problems — they are everyone's responsibility, including yours.

Can AI Be Unfair?

Yes, it can. And not because AI is evil — but because it learns from data.
If that data is unfair or incomplete, AI can make wrong or biased decisions.

Examples:

- If an AI has mostly pictures of light-skinned faces, it may not recognize dark-skinned ones well.
- If an AI was trained mostly on English, it may not understand other languages fairly.
- If a chatbot only learns from angry comments, it may reply rudely!

Think about this: AI is like a mirror — it reflects what we show it. If we give it unfair examples, it can learn bad behavior.

What About Privacy?

Privacy means keeping personal information safe and secure.

Sometimes apps or websites collect:

- Your name and age
- Your location
- What you watch or search
- Who your friends are

If this data is shared or misused, it can be dangerous.
AI companies must ask for permission and protect your data.

Your job: Always check what permissions an app is asking for. Talk to an adult before sharing personal info online.

Who Should Make the Final Decision — AI or Humans?

Imagine this:
A self-driving car has to choose between two roads — one bumpy, one crowded.
- Should it make the decision on its own?
- Or should a human step in?

In important situations like health, safety, or justice, humans should always have the final say. AI can help — but not replace human judgment.

What Can Go Wrong With AI?

When used without care, AI can:
- Spread false news
- Make unfair choices (like rejecting a loan or exam result)
- Be used in war or spying
- Replace people in jobs without warning

This is why countries like India are making AI safety rules, so people use it to build, not break.

AI for Good: What Should We Do?

Let's turn the question around: How can you be a responsible AI user — and maybe one day, a responsible AI creator?

Always ask:

- Who built this AI?
- Where is it getting data from?
- Is it treating everyone equally?

Follow these golden rules:

- Use AI to help, not hurt
- Protect people's privacy
- Ask permission before using data
- Keep learning — so you can ask smart questions!

India's Stand on Ethical AI

India wants AI to be inclusive, safe, and fair.

The government and scientists are working on:

- Making AI available in all Indian languages
- Creating AI ethics guidelines
- Teaching AI responsibly in schools

You are part of this journey — and your values will shape how AI grows in India.

Quick Recap

Question	Answer
Can AI be unfair?	Yes — if it learns from biased data
What is privacy in AI?	Protecting personal info from misuse
Who makes final decisions?	Humans should, especially in serious situations
How to use AI responsibly?	Be fair, ask questions, protect privacy

Try It Yourself!

1. Think of a time when you saw something unfair online. What could have been done differently?
2. Create an "AI Code of Conduct" with 3 simple rules every smart machine should follow.
3. Discuss in class: Should AI be allowed to grade students' exams? Why or why not?

Thought of the Day:

"AI is powerful — but being kind, fair, and thoughtful is even more powerful."

Starter Insight

Abeer Explains:
AI reflects the data it receives.
Amaara Asks:
How can we make sure that data represents everyone fairly?

Chapter 8

Can I Learn AI?

(Yes, You Can!)

You've learned what AI is, how it works, where it lives, and how it helps India grow.

But now comes the most exciting part:
Can YOU learn AI?
Can kids really understand it?
Is AI only for scientists and coders?

The answer is simple: Yes, you can learn AI — and you can start right now!
Let's see how.

You Don't Need to Be a Genius

Some people think that AI is only for "tech experts" or "math wizards." That's not true.

AI is for:

- Curious minds
- Creative thinkers
- Problem solvers
- Everyday students — just like you!

You don't need to know everything about computers. You just need to be willing to ask questions, try new tools, and keep learning.

What Can You Learn First?

Let's break it down into small, fun steps.

1. Learn to Think Like a Computer

- Understand simple steps (called algorithms)
- Break big tasks into smaller parts
- Try board games and logic puzzles to sharpen your thinking

2. Learn Basic Coding

- Use fun websites that teach programming through games:
  - o Scratch (scratch.mit.edu)
  - o Code.org
  - o Blockly Games

These tools let you build your own:

- Animations
- Mini-games
- Storytelling projects — without needing to type complex code!

3. Try AI for Kids

- Tools like Google's Teachable Machine (teachablemachine.withgoogle.com) let you train your own mini-AI using sounds, pictures, or poses
- You can create a model that recognizes your face, voice, or even different types of fruit!

4. Build Projects

- Make a quiz game that uses logic
- Create a chatbot using simple online tools
- Design a robot with cardboard and pretend AI powers

Remember: AI learning is about having fun and being imaginative.

Learn from Around You

You can also learn AI by:

- Watching short videos or animated explainers
- Reading children's books on technology and robots
- Asking questions like:
  - o "How does Google know what I want?"
  - o "How does my phone know where I am?"

Even talking about these things at home or in class helps you grow as an AI learner.

Helpful Books and Resources (Kid-Friendly)

Tool / Website	What It Does
Scratch	Drag-and-drop coding for beginners
Code.org	Game-based coding lessons
Teachable Machine (Google)	Train your own AI models visually
Tynker	Coding games and puzzles for students
YouTube (with guidance)	AI explainer videos (child-safe channels)

Note: Always use the internet with the help of an adult or teacher.

You Can Start an AI Club!

Do you have friends who are also curious about AI?
Start a small AI club in your school or neighborhood. You can:

- Explore fun AI facts together
- Watch videos and discuss ideas
- Do mini projects as a team
- Present your projects on Science Day or AI Day!

Together, you'll grow faster and have more fun.

One Step at a Time

It's okay if you don't understand everything right away. Learning AI is like learning a new sport or language. You get better with practice.

Start with what you love:
- Like drawing? Learn AI art tools.
- Like games? Learn how AI works in gaming.
- Like nature? Use AI to track animals or plants.

AI needs all kinds of talents — and your ideas matter.

Quick Recap

Question	**Answer**
Can kids learn AI?	Yes — through curiosity and practice
Do I need to be a coder?	No — many tools use simple steps and games
How can I start?	Use Scratch, Code.org, or AI explainer tools
What if I'm stuck?	Ask a teacher, parent, or friend for help

Try It Yourself!

1. Visit Scratch or Code.org — create your first animation or game.
2. Write a 5-step algorithm for brushing your teeth or making noodles. That's logic!
3. Interview someone about what they think AI can do in the future.

Final Thought:

"You don't need to be older, richer, or smarter to learn AI.
You just need to be curious. And that journey can start today."

Starter Insight

Abeer Explains:
Every AI expert started by learning basic logic and curiosity.
Amaara Asks:
What problem in your world would you like to solve with AI?

Closing Section: Your AI Adventure Has Just Begun

Congratulations! You've just finished your very first book on Artificial Intelligence — and that's a big achievement.

You now know:

- What AI is and how it works
- Where you use AI every day (often without realizing it!)
- How AI is helping build a better India
- The exciting careers AI is creating
- The importance of fairness, privacy, and ethics
- And most importantly — that you can learn AI too

Remember: AI is not a mystery for grown-ups. It's a tool for you, the next generation of creators, problem-solvers, and change-makers.

India's future in AI isn't just in classrooms or labs — it's in your hands.

Glossary of AI Words (Kid-Friendly Definitions)

Word	Meaning
AI (Artificial Intelligence)	Smart machines that can think, learn, and make decisions like humans
Algorithm	A step-by-step list of instructions to solve a problem
Data	Information that AI uses to learn and make decisions
Machine Learning	When machines learn from examples instead of being told exactly what to do
Neural Network	A computer system made to work like a tiny version of the human brain
Chatbot	A computer program that can talk or chat with people
Bias	When AI treats someone unfairly because of bad or limited data
Privacy	Keeping personal information safe and secure
Prediction	A smart guess made using patterns in data
Coding	Writing instructions that computers can follow
Teachable Machine	A tool where kids can train an AI model using images, sounds, or poses

Activities Section: Learn by Doing

Activity 1: Spot the AI
Write down everything you did today. Circle the ones where AI might have helped you. (Example: YouTube, Google Maps, camera filters)

Activity 2: Become a Data Detective
Ask 3 family members their favorite fruit. Make a list. Which fruit comes up the most?
That's using data — just like AI!

Activity 3: Write Your Own AI Story
Write a short story starting with this line:
"One day, my AI robot made a surprising decision…"
What did it do? Was it helpful? What happened next?

Activity 4: Create Your Own AI Rulebook
Make your "Top 3 Rules" for what every good AI should follow.
(**For example:** Respect privacy, never lie, always be fair.)

Activity 5: Build Your First Algorithm
Write step-by-step instructions for a simple task,

like:

- Making a sandwich
- Getting ready for school
- Drawing a smiley face

That's an algorithm — and it's how AI starts learning!